HARRIET TUBMAN
and the
Underground Railroad

Contents

Written by Philip Steele
Illustrated by Roger Wade Walker

Minty's troubles

Harriet Tubman was born Araminta Harriet Ross to slave parents in about 1822 in Maryland, in the United States of America. She was known to everyone, including her "owners", as Minty. Minty was black and a slave, so she was owned by a white family and could be bought or sold at any time.

Maryland

United States of America

From the age of six, Minty was hired out to work for other people. Her first job was for a local man called James Cook. Her job was to check his **muskrat** traps along the banks of the river. For a little girl, this was cold and muddy work. She was ordered to do the job even when she was suffering from measles. She became very ill so she had to be sent home to her mother until she got better.

Her next job was with a bad-tempered white woman called Miss Susan. Minty had to tidy the house, dust the furniture and rock the cradle, so that Miss Susan's baby didn't wake up. After hours on duty, Minty sometimes fell asleep herself. Then, the baby would wake up and start crying.

Minty was often whipped, so after she was seen taking a lump of sugar from the kitchen table, she ran away and hid with some farm animals in a nearby farm from Friday to Tuesday. She lived off scraps fed to the animals. When she returned, desperately hungry, she was so badly whipped that her back was scarred for the rest of her life.

When Minty was growing up, slavery was still legal in Maryland and across the southern United States. Slaves led very hard lives. They were forced to work for ten to 18 hours a day, either indoors or out in the fields. They weren't paid any wages and were given little food, other than rations of **cornmeal** and pork. Slave families often had a small patch of soil where they could grow vegetables.

Slaves lived on their master's land, generally in small wooden **cabins** that were run-down, overcrowded and unhealthy. The rooms had earthen floors. They were draughty, let the rain in, and were too hot in summer.

Not all African Americans were slaves. Some were set free after they'd worked for an agreed number of years – and their children were born free. But most remained slaves all their lives, with no hope of freedom.

slaves picking cotton

Growing up as a slave

Minty's ancestors came from Ghana in West Africa. Ever since the 1500s, Europeans had shipped Africans held in chains across the Atlantic Ocean to the Caribbean islands or to North or South America. In 1808, the United States stopped **importing** new slaves, but slaves already in the country could still be bought or sold like cattle at public auctions.

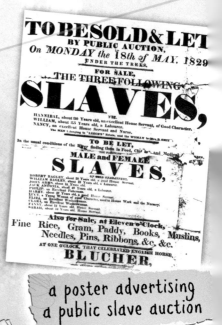

a poster advertising a public slave auction

Minty's father worked on a **plantation**, where he was in charge of cutting down trees and transporting the wood. Minty's mother spent most of her life cooking in kitchens. They met when their owners married and they were brought to the same plantation to work with 15 other slaves.

McDOUGALL FLOUR

Slave families could be broken up and sent to other places whenever their owners wanted. When Minty was just two years old, she and her eight **siblings** were forced to move with their mother to another property about 15 kilometres away, leaving her father behind.

Slave children weren't sent to school and Minty never learnt to read or write. When she wasn't working, she spent a lot of time with her younger brothers and sisters, whom she loved. When she was hired out, she missed her large family terribly.

When Minty was about 13 years old, she had an accident that changed her life forever. On an errand to a local store, she saw a landowner arguing with a young slave who'd run away. When the white man threw a heavy iron weight at the boy, he missed and it hit Minty. She was knocked out and badly injured – for the rest of her life, she had headaches and powerful visions, which she believed were messages giving her the courage to act as she did.

The North Star

Slavery was gradually banned in the northern states of the United States of America between the 1770s and the 1860s. Minty heard more and more stories of slaves escaping to the free states. They "followed the North Star", as its fixed position in the night sky pointed the way to freedom. The whole countryside was buzzing with rumours about escape routes.

slaves following the North Star

Secret networks had already begun to operate long before Minty was born. By the 1830s, these were being nicknamed "the **Underground Railroad**" – after the new railways that were then being built. It has been estimated that by the year 1850, about 100,000 slaves had escaped from the South along this Railroad.

But this was not a real railway. Its "tracks" were roads, rivers and paths. The "carriages" were horses and carts, canoes or rowing boats. The "stations" were hiding places in caves, in country barns, and in the attics and cellars of safe houses in towns. The "**conductors**" were anti-slavery **campaigners**. These free blacks and whites helped the slaves along the way. They led slaves to the next "station" up the line – but they never knew who ran the other sections. That way, it was safer.

In 1849, when Harriet, as she was now known, was about 27, it looked as if she might be sold following the death of her "owner". The owner's wife was left with large debts to pay off, so a sale was one way for her to raise money.

All slaves feared being sold. It meant possibly moving far away and a new owner might be cruel, or work conditions much harsher. Harriet remembered her grief when her sisters were sold to an owner who lived far away, and how her mother had hidden her brother Moses when a man came to buy him. By September of that year, Harriet was desperate and so decided to "follow the North Star" with two of her younger brothers.

Things went badly. The brothers kept arguing about the route and were terrified of the risks they were taking. They decided to turn back even if it meant risking a severe punishment, and they dragged Harriet with them.

Harriet wasn't so easily put off. Within a month, she was making secret plans to set off northwards once again, but this time, on her own.

Before Harriet left, she went over to see her mother in the kitchen where she was working, to say goodbye. But there were too many people around to risk it, so she had to make do with singing a well-known song – and hope that her mother picked up its secret message: *"Farewell, oh farewell, I'll meet you in the morning, I'm bound for the promised land."*

Many Quakers lived in Maryland – they were religious people who had always been against slavery and one Quaker gave Harriet the names of people who could help her along the way. But, to this day, nobody knows for sure the route that Harriet followed or how long it took her.

Harriet had about 150 kilometres to travel. At every moment, she had to watch out for "slave catchers" who could claim big rewards for bringing back escaping slaves. Harriet already knew how to follow back routes through swamps and woods, having spent most of her life working in the countryside. Like other slaves, she now learnt to travel by night when few people were around, or hide under goods on the back of wagons.

At last, she crossed safely into the state of Pennsylvania, where there was no slavery. She felt like she had arrived in heaven!

Working on "the Railroad"

Like many other slaves fleeing from the South, Harriet arrived in the busy city of Philadelphia where anti-slavery campaigns were common. She found work cooking and serving in hotels and saved all the money she could.

Philadelphia

Maryland

United States of America

Baltimore

In December 1850, there was worrying news. Harriet heard that back in Maryland, her niece Kessiah, and Kessiah's two children, were to be sold. Harriet worked out a daring rescue plan and crossed back into Maryland, hiding out in the port of Baltimore.

The slaves were to be auctioned in the town of Cambridge. When the day came, a bid for Kessiah and the children was made and accepted. By the time the auctioneers realised that the bid had been fake, the slaves were nowhere to be seen. They sailed in a small boat all the way to Baltimore, from where Harriet guided them over the state line to Philadelphia and freedom.

Harriet was no longer a passenger on the Underground Railroad – she was a conductor.

During the next ten years, Harriet may have made as many as 13 trips south. She risked her life every time. The Underground Railroad had one important rule: all contacts and routes had to remain secret.

The visions in Harriet's head seemed to make her fearless. Her life became one of secret meetings with strangers and of hiding in backyards. It meant sleeping rough in ditches and snowy woods. Harriet's tough upbringing served her well. When nervous "passengers" panicked, Harriet had to calm them down. Later, many stories were told about Harriet's adventures, the disguises she wore, or how she avoided suspicion by pretending to travel south instead of north.

A law passed in 1850 meant that slave catchers were allowed to operate even in the northern states. Slaves could no longer feel really safe until they had crossed the border into Canada. St Catharines in Ontario became the end station of the Railroad.

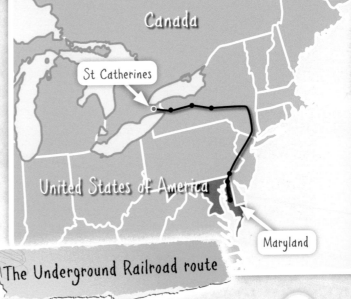

Canada

St Catherines

United States of America

Maryland

The Underground Railroad route

About 70 friends, relations and strangers owed Harriet their freedom, including her own parents. In 1857, her father was accused of helping slaves to escape. This was a serious crime, so Harriet led him and her mother northwards into Canada.

Harriet was just one of many brave conductors on the Railroad. One escaped slave, John P. Parker, led 440 people to safety over the years.

The leading campaigners against slavery soon got to know Harriet and they respected her. In 1860 Harriet was in Troy, New York, when an angry crowd rescued an escaped slave named Charles Nalle, who'd been arrested. The argument about slavery was becoming very heated.

Harriet goes to war

There were growing differences between the regions of the United States of America. The South was a land of farms that used slave labour. The North was a land of new cities and factories, which gave jobs to workers coming into the country from Europe.

In 1861, the southern states decided that they would do better if they broke away from the United States. A **civil war** began between North and South, and in 1863, President Abraham Lincoln declared that he would ban slavery if the North won.

It turned out to be the bloodiest war in American history, killing 625,000 soldiers in all.

Abraham Lincoln, President of the United States of America from 1861 to 1865

soldiers fighting in the American Civil War during 1861 to 1865

24

Harriet already knew which side she was on. In 1862 she had travelled south again, this time to help the northern soldiers. She cooked and worked as a nurse in South Carolina and the army used her to scout out the land and find out where enemy troops were. She knew better than anyone how to travel through the countryside without being spotted.

In June 1863, Harriet took part in an armed raid up the Combahee River, with 300 troops. Over 700 slaves joined them, escaping from their plantations and owners.

Peace and justice

In March 1865, the southern states **surrendered** after a terrible, four-year struggle. The war was over, but President Abraham Lincoln was murdered that April by a southerner who felt bitter about the defeat. A new law was finally agreed in December 1865, **abolishing** slavery in all the United States of America.

a school for slaves that were freed by the American Civil War

Not everything had changed. On the way home from the war, Harriet's arm was injured during a racist incident on a train. Soon laws were being passed to make it hard for black people to have full rights as American citizens. Their struggle for **equality** carried on for over 100 years, but many African Americans were inspired by the example of Harriet Tubman.

Harriet settled down, but she never gave up campaigning for justice. In the 1890s, she spoke out for all women to be given the **vote**. Women respected her because her adventures had proved that she was the equal of any man.

In her old age, Harriet founded a care home for old people, and it was here that she herself died peacefully on 10 March, 1913.

To the end, Harriet told stories of the days of slavery. Her proudest boast was: "I was a conductor on the Underground Railroad for eight years ... I never ran my train off the track and I never lost a passenger."

Glossary

abolishing	getting rid of a law or a custom
cabins	small houses or huts, often made of wood
campaigners	people who organise actions to bring about political or social change
civil war	a war fought between people from the same country
conductors	guards or ticket checkers on a train. (The nickname given to people who helped slaves escape in the United States of America in the 1800s.)
cornmeal	a coarse flour made from maize (sweetcorn)
equality	all people having the same rights
importing	bringing goods – or slaves – into a country
muskrat	a rodent living in the rivers and swamps of North America. It is sometimes caught for its fur.
plantation	a large farm growing rubber, cotton or other crops to sell
siblings	brothers or sisters
surrendered	gave up fighting
Underground Railroad	the nickname given to a network of secret routes across the United States of America in the 1800s. They were used by people escaping from slavery.
vote	making a choice in an election

Index

Harriet Tubman's life

1822 Araminta ("Minty") Ross is born in Maryland as a slave.

1828 Minty is first hired out to work by her "owner".

1844 Minty marries and takes the name Harriet Tubman.

1820   1830   1840   1850   1860

1835 Minty is hit on the head by an iron weight and has headaches and powerful visions for the rest of her life.

1849 Harriet tries to escape with her brothers, then sets out on her own and reaches the free state of Pennsylvania.

1861–5 The American Civil War. Harriet works with the army in South Carolina.

1913 Harriet Tubman dies on 10 March.

1870   1880   1890   1900   1910

1850–60 Harriet becomes a conductor on the Underground Railroad. She leads many more rescue missions from Maryland to Ontario in Canada.

1890s Harriet campaigns for all women to be given the vote.

:: Ideas for reading ::

Written by Linda Pagett B.Ed(hons), M.Ed
Lecturer and Educational Consultant

Learning objectives: use some drama strategies to explore stories and issues; spell unfamiliar words using morphological rules; empathise with characters and debate moral dilemmas portrayed in texts; use syntax, context and word structure to build store of vocabulary; use layout, format, graphics and illustration for different purposes

Curriculum links: Citizenship; History

Interest words: abolishing, North Star, justice, slave, muskrat, scarred, cornmeal, cabin, Ghana, importing, auctions, plantation, network, conductor, carriage, campaigners, Quaker, Civil War, surrendered, abolishing, equality, vote

Resources: whiteboard, globe, an obituary from a newspaper

Getting started

This book can be read over two or more reading sessions.

- Explain to the children that you are going to read a book about slavery in the United States of America during the 1800s. Ask children what they already know about this topic and make a note of any questions they might have.

- Ask one of the children to read the blurb. Discuss what they think the Underground Railroad might be.

- Remind children to use the glossary and word structure to help them guess unfamiliar words, e.g. recognising "under" in "underground".

Reading and responding

- Read pp2–3 together. Ask a child to find Maryland on the map and discuss features of the book that support the reader, e.g. map, illustrations and photographs with captions.

- Ask children to read to p7, and find out what they have learnt so far. Invite children to find Ghana and the Caribbean islands on a globe and trace the journey slave ships made with their fingers.